LONG TO REIGN OVER US
Official Souvenir Album

LONG TO REIGN OVER US

Official Souvenir Album

Royal Collection Trust

To find out more about the
Royal Collection and the Royal Family
go to **www.royalcollection.org.uk**
and **www.royal.gov.uk**

On the late afternoon of 9 September 2015 Her Majesty Queen Elizabeth II became the longest reigning British monarch, passing the previous record held by her great-great-grandmother Queen Victoria, who died in 1901 aged 81 after a reign of 63 years, 7 months and 2 days.

Elizabeth R

I solemnly promise and swear to govern the Peoples of the United Kingdom of Great Britain and Northern Ireland, Canada, Australia, New Zealand and the Union of South Africa, Pakistan and Ceylon, and of my Possessions and the other Territories to any of them belonging or pertaining, according to their respective laws and customs.

I will to my power cause Law and Justice, in Mercy, to be executed in all my judgements.

I will to the utmost of my power maintain the Laws of God and the true profession of the Gospel. I will to the utmost of my power maintain in the United Kingdom the Protestant Reformed Religion established by law. And I will maintain and preserve inviolably the settlement of the Church of England, and the doctrine, worship, discipline, and government thereof, as by law established in England. And I will preserve unto the Bishops and Clergy of England, and to the Churches there committed to their charge, all such rights and privileges as by law do or shall appertain to them or any of them.

The things which I have here before promised, I will perform and keep.

So help me God.

The solemn oath sworn by The Queen during the Coronation Service, and signed using this special pen, summarises Her Majesty's responsibilities as Sovereign. It retains the blue ribbon with which it was originally tied.

Since 1953 the Commonwealth has grown from just 7 nations to 53, representing more than two billion people. The Queen is Head of State of 16 independent sovereign states (including the United Kingdom) among these 53 members. Her Majesty is also Supreme Governor of the Church of England and continues to occupy a unique role as a symbol of unity and strength at the heart of the nation, the Commonwealth and the Anglican Church.

ELIZABETH   REGINA

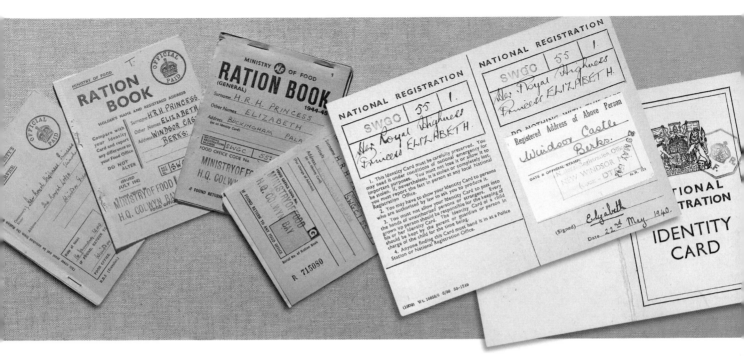

At The Queen's accession in 1952, the country was still recovering from the Second World War: food rationing continued for another two years. Her own ration books – as Princess Elizabeth – are shown above.

During the fifteen years of recovery after 1945 a number of the organisations at the heart of today's national and international life were established.

The UN was founded in 1945, and both the Commonwealth and NATO in 1949. The EEC was created in 1957, merging into the European Union in 1993 (including the UK, which had joined in 1973). The Queen has been involved in each of these continuing developments, understanding the fundamental need for international collaboration to ensure peace in the modern world.

While the Sovereign's traditional formal and ceremonial roles have continued, Her Majesty has also been personally responsible for introducing a number of innovations – such as The Queen's Awards for Enterprise, introduced in 1966, and announced on The Queen's birthday each year.

Many aspects of her role as Sovereign – including her extraordinary sense of duty – were instilled in The Queen by her father and mother, King George VI and Queen Elizabeth. From the start of her reign in 1952, Her Majesty has continued the subtle process of gently adapting the monarchy to changing times, following the examples of her father and grandfather in the first half of the twentieth century.

THE QUEEN'S AWARDS FOR ENTERPRISE

Understanding the increasing need for the monarchy to appear visible, The Queen has sat for more portraits than any previous Sovereign. She has also been photographed – by both professionals and amateurs – on many millions of occasions.

The formal portraits range from Cecil Beaton's 1968 'boat cloak' photograph to Lucian Freud's small oil painting (shown during a final sitting), presented to Her Majesty in 2001 and displayed during the Golden Jubilee.

The first television film about the Royal Family was made in 1969, and 'royal walkabouts' have been a regular part of royal visits since 1970. These have contributed to making The Queen probably the most recognisable figure of the twenty-first century.

CONTINUITY

The Queen was born on 21 April 1926. She was the first child of the Duke of York, the second son of King George V. On the King's death in January 1936 he was succeeded by his eldest son, as King Edward VIII. With the abdication of King Edward (who had no children) and the accession of the Duke of York as King George VI at the end of 1936, Princess Elizabeth became heir presumptive. In a photograph of the Royal Family after the new King's Coronation in May 1937, Princess Elizabeth appears in the centre of the group.

During the Second World War, the young Princess Elizabeth was already involved in the national effort, making her first radio broadcast – on Children's Hour – in October 1940. After the end of hostilities, the Royal Family visited South Africa, where Princess Elizabeth celebrated her 21st birthday in April 1947. In a speech broadcast from Cape Town, she announced:

My whole life whether it be long or short shall be devoted to your service and the service of our great imperial family to which we all belong.

The Princess's engagement, and marriage in November 1947 followed by the birth of Prince Charles in November 1948, provided reassurance of continuity in the royal line. For her son's christening Princess Elizabeth wore Queen Mary's Dorset Bow brooch. This had been a wedding present in 1897 to Queen Mary, who had passed it to her grand-daughter on her marriage.

The Queen's reign commenced
on the death of King George VI, on
6 February 1952. She flew back from
east Africa on the following day,
wearing the brooch given to her by
the children of Southern Rhodesia
on her twenty-first birthday.

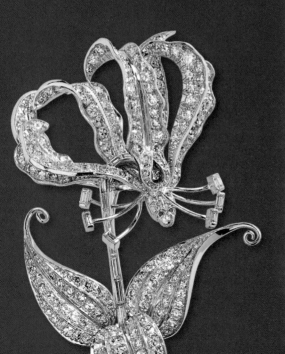

Photographs were soon taken to ensure that the new
monarch's likeness was recorded, and then disseminated

Careful preparation for the Coronation itself – including maintenance of the regalia and production of the new robes to be worn by The Queen – occupied much of the first year of the reign. Her Majesty's spiritual preparation for the service was overseen by the Archbishop of Canterbury (Geoffrey Fisher), who presented this 'Little Book of Private Devotions' at the end of April 1953 to assist The Queen over the following five weeks.

Presented to

Her Majesty the Queen.

with my humble duty,

Geoffrey Cantuar:

April 30 1953.
the first copy.

FOR
THE QUEEN
A
LITTLE BOOK OF
PRIVATE DEVOTIONS
IN PREPARATION FOR
HER MAJESTY'S
CORONATION

TO BE USED
FROM FIRST OF MAY
TO
SECOND OF JUNE
1953

The Queen was crowned on 2 June 1953 at
Westminster Abbey, where every coronation for
the last nine hundred years has taken place. Queen
Elizabeth II is the thirty-ninth Sovereign and sixth
queen to be crowned in her own right at the Abbey.

St Edward's Crown was made for the coronation of Charles II in 1661 and is used only for the act of crowning a new monarch.

When this crown was placed upon The Queen's head, the congregation of 8,251 within the Abbey made their Acclamation by shouting *God Save The Queen*, while the princes and princesses, and the peers and peeresses, simultaneously put on their coronets.

Towards the end of the Coronation
Service, The Queen exchanged
St Edward's Crown for the Imperial
State Crown. This image of the final
procession at the end of the service
reveals the splendour of the royal
regalia and the glittering surface
of The Queen's Coronation dress,
decorated with the national emblems
and symbols of the United Kingdom.

The regalia used at the Coronation represents 'the outward and visible signs of inward and spiritual grace'. The Sovereign's Orb represents the Christian world, while the two sceptres symbolise the Sovereign's spiritual and temporal authority.

The Queen carried both Orb and the Sovereign's Sceptre with Cross out of the Abbey after her Coronation, and bore them during the procession back to Buckingham Palace. Both pieces were made in 1661, but the huge diamond (Cullinan I) was added to the Sceptre in 1911.

Three million people lined the processional route in London. The crowds rapturously cheered The Queen and The Duke of Edinburgh as they travelled in the Gold State Coach, made for George III in 1762. Lining the route or taking part in the procession were 29,200 British, Colonial and Commonwealth troops.

The decision to broadcast the Coronation on television proved a resounding success. An estimated 27 million people – over half the UK population – watched the event, many viewing television for the first time.

In the evening, on radio, The Queen said in a Coronation broadcast to the Nation and the Commonwealth:

As this day draws to a close, I know that my abiding memory of it will be not only the solemnity and beauty of the ceremony, but the inspiration of your loyalty and affection.

The twenty-fifth anniversary of The Queen's accession was celebrated in 1977. To mark the Silver Jubilee a special 25-pence coin was issued. It is shown alongside a miniature book containing The Queen's responses to the loyal addresses presented by both Houses of Parliament.
The high point of the year was the Service of Thanksgiving in St Paul's Cathedral on 7 June.

On the day of the service The Queen wore the Williamson diamond brooch, made in the year of her accession. She met well-wishers in the City of London and was greeted by a further one million people who lined the route of the royal procession back to Buckingham Palace. Across the United Kingdom street parties were held and colourful decorations were on display.

Twenty-five years later, one of the highlights of the Golden Jubilee in 2002 was the 'Party at the Palace', which opened with the National Anthem played by Brian May on Buckingham Palace roof. After the concert The Queen joined performers on stage, including Paul McCartney and Cliff Richard. Throughout the year Her Majesty made a series of tours around the United Kingdom and Commonwealth, journeying over 40,000 miles.

Gifts received by The Queen on her travels included this gold box presented by the Sultan of Brunei.

In the Chapel Royal of St James's Palace, a new stained-glass window was installed. Donated by the chief City Livery Companies, the window includes the names of all the Commonwealth countries within the branches of a blossoming tree.

GRENADA

MALTA

UNITED
KINGDOM

NAMIBIA

E II R

A.D. 2002

PAKISTAN

TONGA

AND ALL MANNER OF

THING SHALL BE WELL

In February 2012 The Queen became only the second British monarch, after Queen Victoria, to reach the sixtieth anniversary of their accession. Events marking the Diamond Jubilee culminated in a weekend of national celebrations during which The Queen attended a Service of Thanksgiving at St Paul's Cathedral on 5 June 2012. She wore the Cullinan III and IV diamond brooch made in 1911 from the magnificent diamond presented by the Government of Transvaal.

The pageant included military, commercial, historic and pleasure craft, making it the largest recorded parade of boats in modern times. Despite the heavy rain – depicted digitally by David Hockney – over a million people lined the Thames to witness the event. On the following day a spectacular concert in front of Buckingham Palace was attended by thousands, and seen on television by millions more around the world.

The most spectacular event of the Diamond Jubilee celebrations was the Thames Diamond Jubilee Pageant on 3 June 2012. The Queen, The Duke of Edinburgh and members of the Royal Family boarded the Royal Barge *Spirit of Chartwell* and were accompanied by a flotilla of 670 vessels.

The investiture ceremony at Caernarvon Castle included many specially designed elements, including the Prince's coronet made by Louis Osman.

The Queen's eldest son and heir, Prince Charles, born in 1948, was created Prince of Wales in 1958 and invested with this title in July 1969. His Royal Highness's formal response to The Queen was:

I, Charles, Prince of Wales, do become your liege man of life and limb and of earthly worship and faith and truth I will bear unto you to live and die against all manner of folks.

28

The Prince of Wales provides increasing support to The Queen in her official duties. In addition to undertaking state and regional visits in her name, he regularly conducts investitures. In February 2015 the author Hilary Mantel was invested by him as a Dame Commander of the British Empire.

Prince Charles is the founder and patron of many charities. Chief among these is the Prince's Trust, founded in 1976 to help young people to access education, training and employment. This plate – made for a gala dinner in 2003 – is decorated with the Prince of Wales feathers and the message 'yes you can'.

29

CONTINUITY

With advances in modern technology, images of The Queen have been more widely disseminated around the globe than those of any previous Sovereign.

Her Majesty's first official photographic sitting – as Queen – took place on 26 February 1952, just 12 days after the accession. Dorothy Wilding, the first female photographer chosen for the task, took a total of 59 shots showing The Queen wearing a variety of different gowns and jewels, including the Diamond Diadem. The Queen's image on postage stamps from 1953 until 1971, including the 2½d and 4d Coronation stamps, and on British bank notes, was based on these photographs. The three-quarter profile image also served as the official portrait of The Queen that was sent to every British Embassy throughout the world.

The Queen's portrait on coinage has been updated five times. Coins using the first portrait, by Mary Gillick, were minted until decimalisation in 1971. The new coins bore the portrait by Arnold Machin; this was later updated by Raphael Maklouf in 1985, by Ian Rank-Broadley in 1997, and most recently by Jody Clark in 2015.

Every year, in her role as Head of State, the Sovereign is driven in state from Buckingham Palace to the Palace of Westminster for the State Opening of Parliament.

Each new session of Parliament opens with The Queen's speech, delivered in the House of Lords to members of both Houses. For the ceremony itself The Queen wears the Imperial State Crown, re-made for King George VI in 1937. For the journey to and from Westminster she wears the Diamond Diadem, made for George IV in 1820.

When The Queen came to the throne, she
assumed the role of Head of the Commonwealth
– a voluntary association of countries formally
constituted in 1949, co-operating for peace,
freedom and the common good. In December
1952 she was photographed at Buckingham
Palace with the chief ministers of the nine
member countries, including Britain's Prime
Minister Sir Winston Churchill.

The Commonwealth bears no resemblance to the empires of the past. It is an entirely new conception built on the highest qualities of the spirit of man: friendship, loyalty, and the desire for freedom and peace. To that new conception of an equal partnership of nations and races I shall give myself heart and soul every day of my life.

The Queen's broadcast to the Commonwealth, made from Government House, Auckland, Christmas Day 1953.

To celebrate Commonwealth Day each spring, The Queen attends an inter-faith service at Westminster Abbey, when the Commonwealth mace is carried before her. Today the Commonwealth has 53 member countries whose citizens total almost one third of the world's population. Their flags decorate the shaft of the ceremonial Commonwealth mace.

The Commonwealth Games are held every four years and are heralded by The Queen's Baton Relay. In October 2013 she placed her message to the 2014 Glasgow Games within the baton at Buckingham Palace. Over 288 days later, and after a journey of over 100,000 miles through 70 nations and territories, The Queen saw the baton again at the opening ceremony.

A new baton is designed for each Games, to reflect the culture and heritage of the hosts.

At recent events (including the Glasgow Games), security passes have been issued for members of the royal party.

Her Majesty is an important presence at the Games. These photographs show The Queen and The Duke of Edinburgh at the Brisbane Games in 1982, and Her Majesty presenting medals at the Kuala Lumpur Games in 1998.

The Sovereign is Commander-in-Chief of the British armed forces. In early 1945 Princess Elizabeth began a period of service in the Auxiliary Territorial Service (ATS). On Remembrance Sunday 1947, when those involved in both world wars were remembered for the first time, Her Royal Highness appeared in uniform at the Cenotaph with her father, King George VI, and Lieutenant Philip Mountbatten (whom she was to marry 11 days later), both in naval uniform.

The Navy is the Senior Service of the armed forces. The Queen, accompanied by The Duke of Edinburgh, travelled to Rosyth Dockyard, Fife, in July 2014 to launch the Navy's biggest ever ship, HMS *Queen Elizabeth*.

At the Sovereign's Parade at the Royal Military Academy, Sandhurst in 2006, The Queen inspected the graduates, including her grandson, Prince William. The Prince went on to serve in the Royal Air Force.

Each year the Sovereign's official birthday in June is marked by The Queen's Birthday Parade on Horse Guards, Whitehall. The Queen takes the salute as the Colour (or standard) of one of the Guards regiments is 'trooped' before her. Her Majesty took the salute on horseback (riding side-saddle) until 1986.

Her mount from 1969 was Burmese, a black mare bred and presented by the Royal Canadian Mounted Police. This one-third-size bronze sculpture of Burmese was presented to The Queen in 1987 by the St John Ambulance Brigade.

Since 1986 The Queen has travelled to and from Trooping the Colour by carriage. In recent times the climax of the day has been the appearance of The Queen and the Royal Family on the balcony of Buckingham Palace to greet the crowd and watch a fly-past by the Royal Air Force.

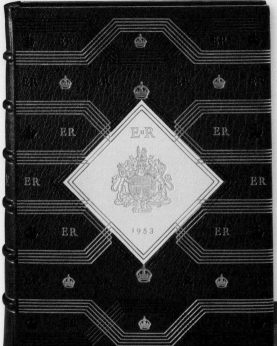

Throughout the United Kingdom, The Queen occupies the role of Defender of the Faith, hence the initials 'FD' – for *Fidei Defensor* – on the national coinage.

At the Coronation, The Queen swore on the Holy Bible to govern with respect for law and justice, applying mercy in her judgements, and to maintain the Laws of God and of the Church of England. This copy of the Coronation Bible was presented to The Queen after the ceremony and is now kept in the Royal Library at Windsor Castle.

Every five years since 1970, The Queen has addressed the General Synod of the Church of England. She is shown here in 2000, when her speech touched upon the work of the Church Urban Fund, of which she is Patron, in helping the poorest in society.

The Queen is in contact with the leaders
of most religious denominations. In February
2012 she was the guest of the Archbishop
of Canterbury, Dr Rowan Williams, at a
multi-faith reception at Lambeth Palace to
mark the Diamond Jubilee. A delegation
of Buddhists presented The Queen with a
miniature silver replica of a stupa, a traditional
Buddhist shrine.

One of the fixed points in The Queen's calendar is the traditional Royal Maundy Service on Maundy Thursday (the day before Good Friday). The service in Westminster Abbey on 10 April 1952 was her first public engagement as Queen.

Her Majesty distributes specially minted silver Maundy Money to elderly individuals in recognition of their service to the Church and community. The numbers of male and female recipients, and the amount they receive, match the Sovereign's age.

In 2012, when The Queen, The Duke of Edinburgh and Princess Beatrice travelled to York Minster, The Queen was in her eighty-fifth year. Therefore each of the 85 male and 85 female recipients was given 85 pence in Maundy coins.

OFFICE
FOR
THE ROYAL MAUNDY

YORK MINSTER

MAUNDY THURSDAY
5TH APRIL 2012

11.00 A.M.

State visits are of crucial importance for strengthening good relations between countries in terms of trade, diplomacy and mutual respect. Incoming visits are hosted by The Queen at one of her official residences. In October 1954 The Queen rode in state with Emperor Haile Selassie of Ethiopia in London, at the start of his visit to the United Kingdom. As a mark of the friendship established during this and subsequent meetings, the Emperor presented The Queen with this silver cross in 1969.

A state visit is also an opportunity for Heads of State to exchange honours. In July 1996 The Queen was photographed beside Nelson Mandela, President of South Africa, on his historic visit to London.

The Queen wears the Order of Good Hope, while President Mandela wears the Order of Merit. These Orders had been bestowed – respectively by the President and The Queen – in the course of Her Majesty's State Visit to South Africa in the previous year.

STATE BANQUET
IN HONOUR OF

THE PRESIDENT
OF
THE FRENCH REPUBLIC
AND
MADAME NICOLAS SARKOZY

WINDSOR CASTLE
WEDNESDAY, 26th MARCH, 2008

The high point of an incoming visit is the banquet given by The Queen in honour of her distinguished guest. Her Majesty always approves the menu and makes a personal inspection of the table as it is laid. The programme for each banquet is decorated with a ribbon in the guest's national colours.

At Windsor the banquet is held in St George's Hall on a 53-metre (174-foot) table, decorated with flowers and adorned with the finest pieces from George IV's Grand Service of silver gilt.

The Queen is Sovereign of all the British Orders of Chivalry. Of these the most senior is the Order of the Garter, founded in 1348 with its spiritual home at St George's Chapel, Windsor Castle. The Garter Star worn by The Queen herself was originally presented to her father in 1923 and was passed to his daughter at the time of her investiture in 1947. Annual Garter services have been held at Windsor since 1954.

The highest honour in Scotland is membership of the Order of the Thistle, founded in 1687. The Queen leads the Order's Services of Thanksgiving, held every other year at St Giles' Cathedral, Edinburgh.

In the course of her reign The Queen has conferred over 400,000 honours and awards. In 2009 she introduced the Elizabeth Cross to provide recognition for the families of armed forces personnel who have died on operations or as a result of an act of terrorism. In September that year she travelled to Catterick Garrison to present this award in person.

The Queen is Patron of over 600 charities and organisations,
all of which benefit from Her Majesty's involvement and
support. In May 2014 she hosted a reception for the
Leonard Cheshire Disability Trust at St James's Palace.
Professor Stephen Hawking was among the guests.

A visit from The Queen will invariably be the cause of much excitement. To mark the opening in December 2013 of the new headquarters of Barnardo's, the children's charity, The Queen and The Duchess of Cornwall, who is Barnardo's President, received flowers from young well-wishers.

For the occasion The Queen wore these aquamarine and diamond clips, which were an eighteenth-birthday gift from her parents. Queen Elizabeth The Queen Mother had also been a Patron of Bernardo's.

In her support for the 'Not Forgotten' Association, The Queen hosted a garden party at Buckingham Palace in June 2014. The charity, founded in 1920, provides help to ex-service personnel. Her Majesty was photographed while greeting the guests.

THE QUEEN and THE DUKE OF EDINBURGH

Opens restored bldg of the Royal College of Pathologists, London SW1.   7

Leave Heathrow Airport to visit Anguilla, Dominica, Guyana, Belize, Cayman Islands   7
        Jamaica, Bahamas and Bermuda

Patron, Rugby Football Union,
opens new East Stand and attends 100th International Rugby Match between

    England and Wales at Twickenham - and the Prince Edward   11

Patron attends recep^n of Royal Coll. of Veterinary Surgeons to mark 150th anniv of Royal Charter   12

opens the new Jewel House, Tower of London   13

give a Reception for winners of the Queen's Award for Export, Technology & Environmental Achievement

visit the Royal Cornwall Museum, Truro   14

Patron, visit the Cinema & Television Benevolent Fund Old People's Home, Wokingham   16
            addresses the Parade

reviews a Parade of Yeomanry to mark the year of the Yeomanry in Windsor Great Park &   17

inaugurates Channel Tunnel, opens Waterloo, Calais & Folkestone Terminals, flypast, speeches   22

give a State Banquet for the President of Zimbabwe   25

entertained at a banquet by the President of Zimbabwe   26

visit Chelsea Flower Show   27

visits RAF Coltishall, Norfolk, recʰ with Royal Saxons; inspects Guard of Honour.   28

visit, Univ of E. Anglia, opens Occupational Therapy & Physiotherapy Building, Norwich   28

attends Epsom Races   29

Each royal engagement, reported to the press through a daily announcement called the Court Circular, is recorded by hand in a ledger. The joint engagements for The Queen and The Duke of Edinburgh in 1994 included an overseas visit, written in red, and the inauguration of the Channel Tunnel (see page 90), underlined in red. These volumes, which date back to the 19th century, are eventually passed to the Royal Archives.

The Queen's year has its regular engagements and ceremonies. In mid-June, Her Majesty leads the Garter Day celebrations at Windsor Castle, dressed in her Garter Robes. At Royal Ascot the five-day race-meeting begins with the royal procession in open landaus.

During Holyrood Week in June or July The Queen takes up residence at the Palace of Holyroodhouse in Edinburgh, her official home in Scotland. In 1976 she was photographed with The Duke of Edinburgh, Princess Margaret and Princess Anne before attending the Royal Company of Archers' Ball.

On Remembrance Sunday each November, The Queen lays a wreath of poppies at the Cenotaph in London to commemorate the sacrifice of all those who have lost their lives in conflicts since the early twentieth century.

Every day The Queen deals with her 'boxes' – the leather-covered cases containing documents and papers for her attention, forwarded by her Private Secretary. Different government departments, and the Scottish and Welsh Assemblies, have their own cases, all of which are now much travelled and well worn.

In addition to official correspondence, The Queen receives a huge amount of private post. In the course of 2006, when she celebrated her eightieth birthday, Her Majesty received around 30,000 birthday cards.

In the Diamond Jubilee year 120,000 messages of congratulation and goodwill arrived from individuals and groups from all over the United Kingdom, the Commonwealth and beyond. Many, like these portraits painted by children in Warrington, were handmade.

INNOVATION

The huge technological advances of the twentieth century have enabled Her Majesty to become the most travelled monarch in history. Her reign began with the six-month Commonwealth Tour of 1953–4 in the course of which The Queen and The Duke of Edinburgh visited 16 countries, travelling 43,618 miles. The majority of the journey was made aboard SS *Gothic*, from which The Queen's personal flag (for each country in which she was also Sovereign) was flown. These included Jamaica, Australia and New Zealand.

The Queen received a rapturous welcome and many gifts on the tour. In New Zealand she was presented with a diamond brooch in the form of a fern, a national emblem, while in Australia she was given a yellow and white diamond brooch in the form of a native wattle-flower.

On 15 May 1954 The Queen and The Duke of Edinburgh returned to London on the newly commissioned Royal Yacht *Britannia*.

During a six-week tour of India and Pakistan in 1961, The Queen and The Duke of Edinburgh visited all the major cities of both countries. In Jaipur, India, she was honoured with a ceremonial ride on an ornately decorated elephant.

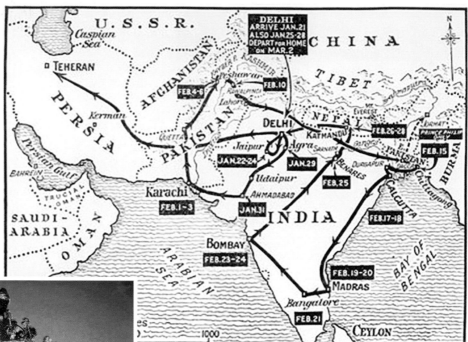

Careful thought and planning went into The Queen's wardrobe for the tour. For a banquet at the presidential residence in Karachi, Her Majesty wore a duchesse satin evening dress in white and emerald – the national colours of Pakistan. To add to the dazzling effect she also wore the Vladimir Tiara hung with the Cambridge Emeralds, from her inherited collection of jewellery.

The Queen became the
first British monarch
ever to visit China when
she and The Duke of
Edinburgh were invited
to pay a State Visit
in October 1986. In
addition to visiting the
Great Wall, The Queen
saw the excavations at
Xi'an, where the famous
terracotta warriors had
been unearthed in the
previous decade.

The visit was of significant diplomatic importance for relations between Britain and China. Numerous gifts were presented to Her Majesty, including this bronze replica model of a chariot and horses found at the Qin Mausoleum, Xi'an.

Between official engagements The Queen took photographs for her personal album.

In May 2011 Her Majesty visited the Republic of Ireland for the first time, heralding a new era in relations between the United Kingdom and Ireland. In consideration for her hosts, The Queen's gown for the State Banquet at Dublin Castle was decorated with an Irish harp in crystals and more than two thousand silk shamrocks sewn on by hand.

The Queen was presented with a specially bound facsimile of an Irish primer first given to Elizabeth I.

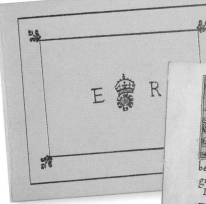

In Dublin The Queen attended a ceremony with Mary McAleese, the Irish President, at which they both laid wreaths at the Irish War Memorial Gardens, dedicated to the 49,400 Irish soldiers who died in the First World War.

On the final day of The Queen's four-day tour she visited one of Ireland's most famous food-markets, the English Market at Cork. Photographs of her sharing a joke with the market traders received international coverage.

The Queen's regular regional visits are of great importance. They are a means of enabling as many people as possible to have contact with their Head of State. They also provide a valuable focus to the place or organisation visited. In 1961 Her Majesty helped to bring attention to a Government Training Centre at Felden, Northern Ireland.

In 2002, as part of her Golden Jubilee Tour, she opened the new Sunderland to Newcastle Metro. Ten years later, she waved the starting flag for the Sport Relief run at Salford.

A wide variety of gifts have been presented
to The Queen in the course of these visits.
At Aldgate East Underground Station in
2010 she was presented with a specially
produced London Underground sign.

In 2002, to mark her dedication of the
Gateshead Millennium Bridge on Tyneside,
The Queen was given this glass vase,
made by a local glass-maker.

The Queen's wardrobe is designed to complement each engagement and ensure that she is clearly visible. Dresses, coats, hats and accessories are all set out by Angela Kelly, Her Majesty's Personal Advisor and Senior Dresser. The Queen makes her own choice of jewellery for each day's events. For her visit to Nottingham in the company of The Duchess of Cambridge during the Diamond Jubilee in 2012, she chose one of the diamond bow brooches made for Queen Victoria in 1858.

Many of The Queen's
official tours between 1954
and 1997 were undertaken
on the Royal Yacht
Britannia. On her visit to
Canada in 1959 *Britannia*
docked on the Canadian
shore opposite Detroit for
The Queen and The Duke
of Edinburgh to greet
the crowds from an open
car. In 1977 The Queen
travelled on a rather swifter
form of transport when
she returned from her tour
of Canada and the West
Indies by Concorde.

The Queen and The Duke of Edinburgh appear at the windows of the Royal Train at the end of a regional visit to Derbyshire in 1957. The train includes catering and office facilities to allow The Queen to continue working while travelling.

The Queen's official car has changed during her reign but the detachable mascot on the bonnet – a silver figure of St George and the Dragon, designed by Edward Seago – has remained in use since the late 1940s. The Queen and The Duke of Edinburgh also travel by helicopter, for which there are landing places close to all the royal residences.

INNOVATION

The Queen's first Christmas Day message was broadcast by radio from Sandringham in 1952. From 1957 her Christmas message has also been televised. New technology has continued to be embraced, with the broadcast now being streamed over the internet. In 2012 it was recorded in 3D.

The tradition of the Christmas broadcast began in 1932 with The Queen's grandfather, King George V. His words – *I speak now from my home and from my heart to you all* – set the tone for what continues to be a personal message from the Sovereign.

To widen public access to the official activities of the Royal Family and Household, The Queen launched the British Monarchy's official website (www.royal.gov.uk) in 1997. In 2007 the official British Monarchy YouTube channel was unveiled, followed by a Royal Twitter account in 2009 and Flickr and Facebook pages in 2010. The Queen sent the first royal tweet under her own name at the Science Museum in October 2014.

To keep pace with the rapidly changing modern world, since 1952 the Royal Household has itself changed in a number of ways. In 2012 those working at Buckingham Palace were photographed with The Queen and The Duke of Edinburgh to celebrate Her Majesty's Diamond Jubilee. Household employees at the different royal residences provide The Queen with essential support, to enable Her Majesty to serve the nation and its people.

The Household was among the first to embrace technological advances. This early personal computer, a gift to The Queen from the US government in 1983, was immediately put to use.

The Household now attracts young people with diverse backgrounds and interests. Career Days are held in the different residences, and training is provided in a very wide variety of skills and specialisms.

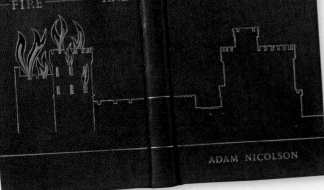

FIRE — AND — RESTORATION

ADAM NICOLSON

A major fire at Windsor Castle on 20 November 1992 caused serious damage to many of the State and Private Apartments. A watercolour by Alexander Creswell shows the charred remains of the Crimson Drawing Room. The damaged areas were restored over the following five years, as described in this publication, specially bound for The Queen in the Royal Bindery at Windsor.

In 1993, to fund restoration work on Windsor Castle, which included returning the Crimson Drawing Room and other apartments to their former glory, The Queen decided to open Buckingham Palace to the public for the first time.

The State Rooms have been open every summer since then, with a different special display each year. To mark the sixtieth anniversary of The Queen's Coronation in 2013, her Coronation Robes were displayed in the Palace Ballroom.

An important innovation was the opening in 1962 of a gallery at Buckingham Palace to display items from the Royal Collection. In 2002 The Prince of Wales, Chairman of the Royal Collection Trustees, greeted The Queen prior to the opening of the new Queen's Gallery in London.

A similar gallery at the Palace of Holyroodhouse, Her Majesty's official residence in Scotland, also opened in 2002.

In addition to temporary exhibitions, Royal Collection Trust runs education programmes, seeks to increase access through new technology, and has a dedicated staff of curators and conservators who care for the many hundreds of thousands of items in the Collection.

MOMENTS TO REMEMBER

News of the success of the British Mount Everest Expedition on 29 May 1953 was announced in London on the morning of The Queen's Coronation. All 34 members of the expedition, including Sir Edmund Hillary and Tenzing Norgay who were the first to reach the previously unconquered summit, were awarded the newly minted Coronation Medal.

The Queen first addressed the General
Assembly of the United Nations on
21 October 1957. On 6 July 2010,
over fifty years later, she addressed the
UN for a second time. In his welcome
Ban Ki-moon, the UN Secretary-
General, acknowledged The Queen's
importance as a figure of continuity:
*In a changing and churning world, you are an
anchor for our age.*

In 1966 Britain hosted the FIFA World Cup. The final was played at Wembley Stadium on 30 July. Amid great jubilation The Queen presented the cup to Bobby Moore, the captain of the victorious England team. Stamps produced to coincide with the tournament were re-issued with the legend 'England Winners'.

Her Majesty was among 50 world leaders who contributed messages of goodwill that were deposited on the moon's surface during the historic Apollo 11 moon landing, 20 July 1969. The Queen received the crew members, Michael Collins, Neil Armstrong and Edwin 'Buzz' Aldrin, at Buckingham Palace three months later.

Draft Message from Her Majesty The Queen to be deposited on the Moon by the Apollo 11 Astronauts.

"On behalf of the British people I salute the skill and courage which have brought man to the moon. May this endeavour increase the knowledge and well-being of mankind."

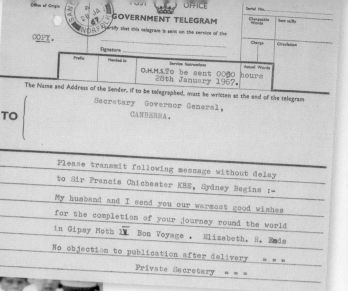

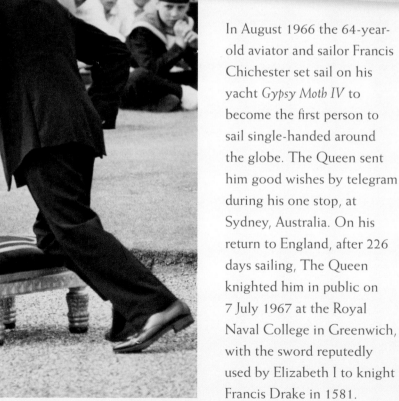

In August 1966 the 64-year-old aviator and sailor Francis Chichester set sail on his yacht *Gypsy Moth IV* to become the first person to sail single-handed around the globe. The Queen sent him good wishes by telegram during his one stop, at Sydney, Australia. On his return to England, after 226 days sailing, The Queen knighted him in public on 7 July 1967 at the Royal Naval College in Greenwich, with the sword reputedly used by Elizabeth I to knight Francis Drake in 1581.

A significant stage of the transition from Empire to a Commonwealth of self-governing nations was reached in 1975 when – on the advice of ministers in the respective countries – The Queen instituted the Order of Australia (left) in February, followed by The Queen's Service Order, New Zealand (right), in March. In Canada a similar change had already been heralded by the introduction of the Order of Canada (centre) in 1967, and the Order of Military Merit in 1972. The Queen is Sovereign of all of these orders.

The Channel Tunnel was officially opened by The Queen and President Mitterand of France in May 1994, after many years of discussion and engineering work.

A piece of the inaugural ribbon cut by The Queen and the President is kept as a souvenir, together with the gilt commemorative medal.

In 1999 two important steps were taken in the devolution of parliamentary power from Westminster. In May The Queen signed a special edition of the 'First Words' Act inaugurating a new relationship between Westminster and the Welsh Assembly in Cardiff.

In July she attended the opening ceremony of the Scottish Parliament in Edinburgh. The Scottish Crown, made for James V of Scotland in 1540, was brought from Edinburgh Castle to the chamber.

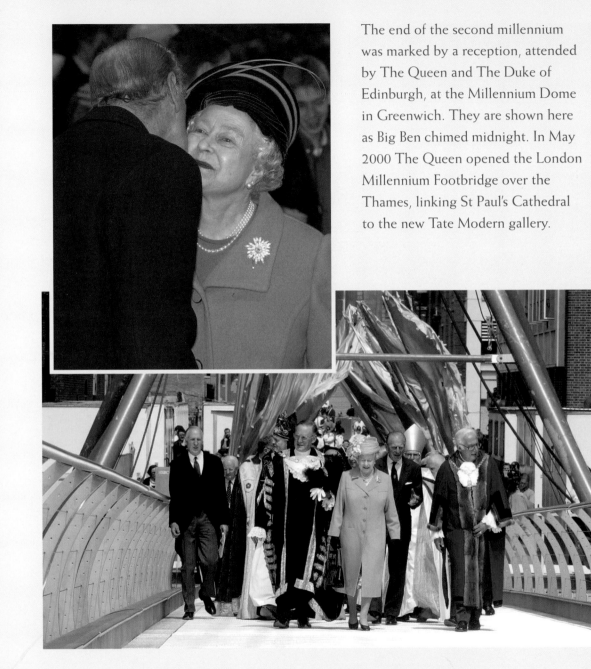

The end of the second millennium was marked by a reception, attended by The Queen and The Duke of Edinburgh, at the Millennium Dome in Greenwich. They are shown here as Big Ben chimed midnight. In May 2000 The Queen opened the London Millennium Footbridge over the Thames, linking St Paul's Cathedral to the new Tate Modern gallery.

The Queen's arrival at the London 2012 Olympics Opening Ceremony was preceded by a film in which she appeared to join the fictional character James Bond to make a parachute jump into the stadium (see pages 82–3). For the occasion two identical dresses were made, one worn by Her Majesty's body double. The Queen herself wore the diamond brooch made for Queen Adelaide in 1831.

The Queen has been a keen rider since her early childhood: in 1960 she was photographed riding along the racecourse at Ascot.

As owner and breeder she has also been a keen participant in 'the sport of kings'. Horses owned by Her Majesty have won over 1,500 races. In 1978 she shared a joke with Willie Carson, the jockey who had ridden her horse Dunfermline to victory in both the Epsom Oaks and the St Ledger Stakes in 1977, wearing the royal racing colours – purple body with gold braid, scarlet sleeves and black velvet cap.

In June 2013 The Queen's filly Estimate was victorious in Royal Ascot's Gold Cup – the first time in the race's 207-year history that it had been won by a reigning monarch. The Queen watched the final moments from the Royal Box with her Racing Manager, John Warren. The cup was presented to Her Majesty by The Duke of York.

In the course of her long reign, The Queen has met more Heads of State than any other British monarch.

In 1957 Her Majesty paid her first State Visit to the United States, where she was the guest of Dwight D. Eisenhower, Supreme Commander of Allied Forces in Europe during the Second World War, Supreme Commander of NATO from 1951, and President of the United States from 1953 to 1961. The Queen wore this Hardy Amies gown to the State Banquet at the White House on 20 October 1957.

Over the years The Queen has received many Presidents of the United States on their visits to Britain. President John F. Kennedy was her guest at Buckingham Palace on 5 June 1961, while in 2011 she held a State Banquet to honour President Barak Obama's State Visit. Her own visits to the USA have been marked with honours. In May 1991 The Queen was the first British monarch to address the House of Congress.

The Queen has also met many of the statesmen and women who are considered seminal figures in the history of the modern world.

In April 1960 Her Majesty received President Charles de Gaulle of France; and in 1986 her meeting with the leader of the People's Republic of China, Deng Xiaoping, was seen as especially significant.

On the Queen's State Visit to India in November 1983, she was the guest of India's first woman Prime Minister, Mrs Indira Gandhi.
The following year Her Majesty and The Duke of Edinburgh were guests of King Hussein and Queen Noor of Jordan. The official programme of events for the State Visit was bound in red leather and stamped with the Jordanian crown.

The momentous events of 1989 included the April visit of President Gorbachev of the USSR to Windsor Castle as The Queen's guest. In early November of the same year the wall dividing East and West Berlin was demolished and – like many Western Heads of State – The Queen was sent a portion of the demolished wall by the people of Germany. The Cold War was at an end.

The break-up of the former Soviet Union saw new leaders emerge in the countries of Eastern Europe. In March 1996 The Queen was awarded the Order of the White Lion by President Vaclev Havel on the occasion of her visit to the Czech Republic, which culminated in a banquet at Prague Castle.

In April 1991 The Queen had welcomed the President of the Republic of Poland, Lech Walesa, with a carriage ride at Windsor on the first day of his State Visit to Britain.

The Queen has made several visits to the Vatican. In October 1980 she was received by and exchanged gifts with Pope John Paul II.

More recently, in April 2014 The Queen met Pope Francis, who presented this lapis lazuli orb, topped by a silver cross, as a gift to The Queen's great-grandchild, Prince George of Cambridge.

The Order of Merit, founded by King Edward VII in 1902, is in the sole gift of the Sovereign and is awarded to those who have rendered exceptionally meritorious service. In November 1983, at a special ceremony at the Rashtapati Bhavan, Mother Theresa of Calcutta became an Honorary Member of the Order.

Over her long reign, Her Majesty has been served by 12 Prime Ministers. Her first Prime Minister was Sir Winston Churchill, with whom she was photographed in 1954, while waiting (with Prince Charles and Princess Anne) for the return of Queen Elizabeth the Queen Mother from her tour of Canada and America.

In December 1985, to celebrate the 250th anniversary of 10 Downing Street becoming the Prime Minister's London residence, The Queen attended a dinner hosted by Margaret Thatcher. The photograph (above right) shows Her Majesty with six of her Prime Ministers: from the left, James Callaghan, Alec Douglas-Home, Margaret Thatcher, Harold Macmillan, Harold Wilson and Edward Heath. On that occasion The Queen wore a chiffon gown (at left) by Hardy Amies.

In the Diamond Jubilee year, 2012, David Cameron hosted a luncheon where The Queen and former Prime Ministers John Major, Tony Blair and Gordon Brown were guests.

Since its inception in 1946, the annual Royal Film Performance has raised funds for the Cinema and Television Benevolent Fund. Over the years many stars have been presented to The Queen at these events, including Marilyn Monroe in 1956.

At the premiere of Laurence Olivier's *Richard III* in 1955, all eyes turned to The Queen and The Duke of Edinburgh as they entered the Royal Box at the Empire Theatre, Leicester Square.

The Queen has been a frequent attender of the Royal Variety Performance since 1949. Initiated in 1912, the annual event raises funds for the Entertainment Artistes' Benevolent Fund. Being presented to The Queen is a special moment for entertainers.

In 1965 the singer Shirley Bassey lined up backstage alongside the comedians Peter Cook and Dudley Moore.

International stars are a regular feature of the show. In 2009 Lady Gaga was among the cast.

Dame Carol Ann Duffy is The Queen's sixth Poet Laureate. In addition to being closely involved in the annual award of The Queen's Gold Medal for Poetry, Duffy wrote 'The Crown' to mark the sixtieth anniversary of The Queen's Coronation in 2013. The poem was lettered by the textual artist Stephen Raw.

The Queen has supported music and poetry throughout her reign. In June 1953 she attended the premiere of Benjamin Britten's *Gloriana*, commissioned by the Royal Opera House to celebrate her Coronation, which had taken place just six days before. In 2005 she instituted The Queen's Medal for Music, which she awarded to the soprano Dame Emma Kirkby in 2011, watched by Master of the Queen's Music, Sir Peter Maxwell Davies.

THE CROWN

TRANSLATES
a WOMAN to a QUEEN — ENDLESS
GOLD, circling
itself, an like a
WELL.

fathomless, for the YEARS to DROWN IN —
HISTORY'S BRIDE,
ANOINTED, blessed, for a
CROWNING.

ONE
HEAD ALONE CAN KNOW
ITS WEIGHT, on
THRONE, in PAGEANTRY. AND FEEL
IT STILL,
in private SPACE, WHEN IT'S
LIFTED:

Not A HOLLOW
THING, but A MEASURING; NO HALO,
TREASURE, but A VALUING:
DECADES A DUTY. TIME-GIFTED, the CROWN
IS OLD LIGHT.

JOURNEYING
from SKULLS
of KINGS to LIVING
QUEEN. ITS JEWELS GLOW,
VIRTUES;

LOYALTY'S
RUBY, blood-DEEP; Sapphire's ICE
RESILIENCE; EMERALD
EVERGREEN; the Sly PEARL,
HUMILITY.

My whole LIFE,
WHETHER IT BE LONG or SHORT,
DEVOTED to YOUR
SERVICE.

NOT Lightly WORN.

Throughout her reign, The Queen has been supported by her husband, Prince Philip, The Duke of Edinburgh. Their wedding took place at Westminster Abbey on 20 November 1947 and was followed by a honeymoon at Broadlands in Hampshire, the home of Prince Philip's uncle, Lord Mountbatten. Sixty years later The Queen and Prince Philip returned to Broadlands to be photographed in the same pose. A service to celebrate their Diamond Wedding Anniversary was held in Westminster Abbey in 2007.

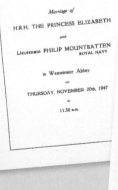

Marriage of
H.R.H. THE PRINCESS ELIZABETH
with
Lieutenant PHILIP MOUNTBATTEN
ROYAL NAVY
in Westminster Abbey
on
THURSDAY, NOVEMBER 20th, 1947
at
11.30 a.m.

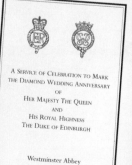

A SERVICE OF CELEBRATION TO MARK
THE DIAMOND WEDDING ANNIVERSARY
OF
HER MAJESTY THE QUEEN
AND
HIS ROYAL HIGHNESS
THE DUKE OF EDINBURGH

Westminster Abbey

Monday 19 November 2007
11.30 a.m.

Princess Elizabeth's first child, Prince Charles, was born at Buckingham Palace on 14 November 1948. The King and Queen gave their daughter this flower basket brooch to celebrate. Princess Elizabeth wore the brooch in the first photographs of mother and child, taken by Cecil Beaton.

In 2013 she wore the same brooch at the Christening of her great-grandson, Prince George, the first child of The Duke and Duchess of Cambridge.

In August 2000 Queen
Elizabeth The Queen Mother
celebrated her hundredth
birthday. The Queen's
personalised telegram was
delivered to Clarence House
before the Royal Family
gathered at Buckingham Palace
for lunch and an extremely
popular balcony appearance.

On your 100th Birthday
all the family join with me
in sending you our loving
best wishes for this special day

Lilibet

BUCKINGHAM PALACE
LONDON SW1A 1AA

ROYAL MAIL

Her Majesty Queen Elizabeth The Queen Mother
Clarence House
St. James's
London
SW1A 1BA

The Queen celebrated her eightieth birthday at Windsor in April 2006. This portrait was taken by the veteran press photographer Jane Bown, who was born one year before The Queen.

In September 2015, the point at which Her Majesty became the longest reigning monarch in British history, she was 89 years of age and is continuing the duty of service she undertook on her accession over 63 years ago. Long live The Queen!

Illustrations

Unless otherwise stated, all illustrations are Royal Collection Trust / © HM Queen Elizabeth II 2015. Items with RA references are Royal Archives / © HM Queen Elizabeth II 2015. Royal Collection Trust is grateful for permission to reproduce those items listed below for which copyright is not held by Royal Collection Trust or Royal Archives.

Front cover:
• *The Queen and The Duke of Edinburgh leaving for the State Opening of Parliament in London, 27 May 2015.* Photograph by Stephen Lock / i-Images

Back cover:
• *The Royal Family on the balcony of Buckingham Palace following the Trooping the Colour Ceremony, 13 June 2015.* Photograph by Anwar Hussein, Press Association/ EMPICS Entertainment

Endpapers:
• The Queen's bookplate, designed by Will Carter, 1958

Half-title page:
• *The Queen in the Gold State Coach on her way to her Coronation at Westminster Abbey. 2 June 1953.* A still from the colour film *A Queen is Crowned,* 1953, ITV/REX Shutterstock.
• *The Queen and The Duke of Edinburgh in the Gold State Coach on their way to the Service of Thanksgiving at St Paul's Cathedral to mark the Golden Jubilee, 4 June 2002.* Press Association Images

Opposite title page:
• *The Queen in her Golden Jubilee Year, 2002.* Photograph by Mark Lawrence, copyright www.royalimages.co.uk

Title page:
• Andy Warhol, from: *Reigning Queens (Royal Edition): Queen Elizabeth II of the United Kingdom,* 1985. Screenprint in colour with 'diamond dust', (RCIN 507013.d) © 2015 The Andy Warhol Foundation for the Visual Arts, Inc. / Artists Rights Society (ARS)

p. 5
• *The Queen at Canterbury Cathedral, 26 March 2015.* Photography by Arthur Edwards. Press Association Images

p. 6
• The Coronation Oath. © The National Archives
• The Coronation Pen used to sign the Oath (RCIN 39431)

p. 7
• Princess Elizabeth's ration books and identity card (RA GVI/PRIV/PERS and RA PS/GVI/C233/04 and 12–15). Crown Copyright material reproduced with the permission of the controller of TSO and The Queen's Printer for Scotland

p. 8
• Studio Lisa, *King George VI and Princess Elizabeth,* (RCIN 2935355). Copyright reserved
• Emblem of The Queen's Award for Enterprise

p. 9
• Cecil Beaton, *HM Queen Elizabeth II, 16 October 1968.* Gelatin silver print (RCIN 2999826)
• *Lucian Freud at work on his portrait of HM Queen Elizabeth II, 2001.* Photography by David Dawson (RCIN 2584774). Photograph © David Dawson

CONTINUITY

pp. 10–11
• *The Queen, the Prince of Wales and The Duchess of Cornwall on the balcony of Buckingham Palace during the Diamond Jubilee celebrations, 5 June 2012.* Press Association Images

p. 12
• *King George VI, Queen Elizabeth, Princess Elizabeth and Princess Margaret in their Coronation robes, May 1937.* Photograph by Dorothy Wilding (RCIN 2999915). Reproduced by kind permission of Will & Georgina Hustler
• Princess Elizabeth's Coronet, Garrard, 1937 (RCIN 75056)

p. 13
• *King George VI, Queen Elizabeth, Princess Elizabeth, The Duke of Edinburgh and Prince Charles, Buckingham Palace, 15 December 1948.* (RCIN 2814350)
• Queen Mary's Dorset Bow brooch, Carrington & Co., 1893 (RCIN 200190)

p. 14
• The Flame Lily brooch, 1947 (RCIN 250033)
• *The Queen arriving at London Airport from Kenya, 9 February 1952* (RCIN 2999978). Copyright Reserved/Royal Collection Trust

p. 15
• *The Imperial State Crown being adjusted in preparation for the Coronation, 1953* (RCIN 2081551)
• *Embroideress at work on the Coronation Robe, 11 February 1953* (RCIN 2002692)
• Geoffrey Fisher, *A Little Book of Private Devotions in preparation for Her Majesty's Coronation,* 1953 (RCIN 1006833)

p. 16
• *The moment of Crowning, Westminster Abbey, 2 June 1953* (RCIN 2584766)

p. 17
• St Edward's Crown, 1661 (RCIN 31700)

p. 18
• *The Queen in procession out of Westminster Abbey.* A still from *A Queen is Crowned,* 1953. ITV/REX Shutterstock

p. 19
• The Sovereign's Sceptre with Cross, 1661 (RCIN 31712)
• The Sovereign's Orb, 1661 (RCIN 31718)

p. 20
• *The Coronation procession passes through Trafalgar Square, 2 June 1953.* Press Association Images
• *The Queen and The Duke of Edinburgh in the Gold State Coach in procession to Westminster Abbey.* Still from *A Queen is Crowned,* 1953. ITV/REX Shutterstock

p. 21
• *The Queen, The Duke of Edinburgh, Prince Charles and Princess Anne on the balcony of Buckingham Palace on the day of the Coronation, 2 June 1953* (RCIN 2584772)
• Images from the BBC Coronation television broadcast. Press Association Images
• *The Sheriff of Nottingham with old-age pensioners watches the televised broadcast of The Queen's Coronation.* Local World/REX Shutterstock

p. 90
• *The Queen and President Mitterand of France at the official opening of the Channel Tunnel, 6 May 1994.* Photograph by Tim Ockenden (RCIN 28999999). Press Association Images
• Coloured lace ribbon with gilt medal commemorating the inauguration of the Channel Tunnel, 6 May 1994 (RCIN 63720, 446152)

p. 91
• *The Queen signs a special edition of the 'First Words' Act before presenting the bound volume to the Welsh Assembly and its Members, 26 May 1999.* Gareth Everatt/Getty Images
• *The Queen looks over the Scottish Crown during the opening of the Scottish Parliament in the parliament chamber, Edinburgh, 1 July 1999.* Press Association Images
• The Scottish Crown, 1540. © Crown Copyright, reproduced courtesy of Historic Scotland

p. 92
• *The Duke of Edinburgh and The Queen during the New Year's Eve celebration at the Millennium Dome, 1 January 2000.* Press Association Images
• *The Queen and The Duke of Edinburgh, the Mayor of Southward (Charles Cherrill) and the Lord Mayor of London (Clive Martin), walk across the newly opened London Millennium Footbridge, 9 May 2000.* Press Association Images

p. 93
• *The Queen arrives at the Opening Ceremony to the London 2012 Olympics, 27 July 2012.* Press Association Images
• Angela Kelly, salmon pink silk and lace dress, embroidered with sequins and gold thread, for the London 2012 Olympics Opening Ceremony. © HM Queen Elizabeth II
• The Queen Adelaide diamond brooch, 1831, remodelled 1858 (RCIN 250508)

p. 94
• *The Queen riding at Ascot, June 1960* (RCIN 2006975). Royal Collection Trust/All Rights Reserved
• *The Queen with Willie Carson, Newmarket racecourse, 18 April 1978.* PA/PA Press Association Images
• The Queen's racing colours

p. 95
• *The Queen and her racing manager John Warren watch Estimate win the Gold Cup at Royal Ascot, 20 June 2013.* Press Association Images
• The Ascot Gold Cup 2013, won by Estimate (RCIN 98805)

• *The Queen is presented with the Gold Cup by The Duke of York, Ascot, 20 June 2013.* Press Association Images

p. 96
• *The Queen with President Eisenhower at the White House, 20 October 1957* (RCIN 1381108i)
• Hardy Amies grey satin dress with full skirt, embroidered with gold bugles and grey beads and crystals (RCIN 100070)

p. 97
• *The Queen and President John Kennedy at Buckingham Palace, 5 June 1961.* Press Association Images
• *The Queen and President Barack Obama at Buckingham Palace, 24 May 2011.* Press Association Images
• *The Queen applauded by Vice-President Dan Quayle and House Speaker Thomas Foley before her address to the US Congress, Washington DC, 16 May 1991.* Press Association Images

p. 98
• *The Queen and President Charles de Gaulle of France on their processional drive to Buckingham Palace, 5 April 1960.* Press Association Images
• *The Queen meeting Deng Xiaoping in Beijing, 14 October 1986.* Press Association Images

p. 99
• *The Queen and Mrs Indira Gandhi at Hyderabad House in New Delhi, 18 November 1983.* Photograph by David Levenson/Getty Images
• *The Queen and The Duke of Edinburgh with King Hussein and Queen Noor beside the Dead Sea during the State Visit to Jordan, 28 March 1984.* Press Association Images
• Jordanian programme for the State Visit

p. 100
• *The Queen and President Gorbachev of the USSR during his visit to Windsor Castle, April 1989.* Photograph courtesy Baylis Media Ltd. Press Association Images
• Fragment of the Berlin Wall, demolished 1989 (RCIN 37064)

p. 101
• The Order of the White Lion, presented to The Queen in 1996, (RCIN 250990)
• *The Queen arrives with President Havel at a State Banquet in Prague Castle, during her visit to the Czech Republic, 27 March 1996.* © Ian Jones. Press Association Images
• *The Queen with the President of Poland, Lech Walesa, at the start of his State Visit to Britain, 23 April 1991.* Press Association Images

p. 102
• *The Queen and The Duke of Edinburgh exchange gifts with Pope John Paul II during a visit to the Vatican, 17 October 1980.* Photograph by Anwar Hussein. Press Association Images
• *The Queen and Pope Francis on her official visit to Vatican City, 3 April 2014.* ddp USA/REX Shutterstock
• Lapis lazuli orb surmounted by a silver cross presented by Pope Francis as a gift for Prince George. Royal Collection Trust/All Rights Reserved

Page 103
• *The Queen presenting the Order of Merit to Mother Theresa of Calcutta at the Rashtrapati Bhavan in New Delhi, 24 November 1983.* Press Association Images
• The Order of Merit Lady's Badge

p. 104
• *The Queen (with Prince Charles and Princess Anne) talks to Sir Winston Churchill while awaiting the arrival of Queen Elizabeth The Queen Mother at Waterloo Station on her return from visiting Canada and America, 24 November 1954.* © Topham Picturepoint

p. 105
• *Prime Minister Margaret Thatcher is joined by The Queen and five former Prime Ministers to celebrate the 250th anniversary of 10 Downing Street as the Prime Minister's official London residence, 4 December 1985.* Press Association Images
• *The Queen with David Cameron, (far left) and former Prime Ministers Sir John Major, Tony Blair and Gordon Brown, at a Diamond Jubilee luncheon, 10 Downing Street, 24 July 2012.* Press Association Images
• Hardy Amies cream chiffon gown with a bodice embroidered with poppies (RCIN 100079)

p. 106
• *The Queen and The Duke of Edinburgh enter the Royal Box for the Royal Film Performance of Richard III, 15 December 1955.* Press Association Images
• *The Queen greets Marilyn Monroe at the Royal Film Performance of* The Battle of the River Plate, *29 October 1956.* Press Association Images

p. 107
• *The Queen talks to Shirley Bassey with Peter Cook and Dudley Moore, 9 November 1965.* Press Association Images
• *The Queen meets the singer Lady Gaga at the Royal Variety Performance, Blackpool, 8 December 2009.* Photograph by Leon Neal © Agence France-Presse
• The Royal Variety Performance programme for 2009

p. 108
• *The Queen and The Duke of Edinburgh at the premiere of the opera* Gloriana, *8 June 1953* (RCIN 2002638)

• The Queen's Medal for Music, designed by Bethan Williams. Royal Collection Trust/All Rights Reserved
• *The Queen presents The Queen's Medal for Music to Dame Emma Kirkby, watched by the Master of The Queen's Music Sir Peter Maxwell Davies, 2 June 2011.* Press Association Images

p. 109
• Carol Ann Duffy, *The Crown*, 2013, lettered by textual artist Stephen Raw (RCIN 454295)

p. 110
• *Princess Elizabeth and The Duke of Edinburgh on their honeymoon, November 1947* (RCIN 2584776). Press Association Images
• *Diamond Wedding Anniversary photograph of The Queen and The Duke of Edinburgh, November 2007.* Photograph by Tim Graham (RCIN 2937789) Getty Images
• Order of Service for the Marriage Ceremony of Princess Elizabeth and Lieutenant Philip Mountbatten, 20 November 1947 (RA F&V/Weddings/1947QEII)
• Order of Service for the Diamond Wedding Anniversary of The Queen and The Duke of Edinburgh, Westminster Abbey, 2007. Copyright the Dean and Chapter of Westminster

p. 111
• *Princess Elizabeth with the infant Prince Charles, 14 December 1948.* Photograph by Cecil Beaton (RCIN 2999884)
• Flower basket brooch, rubies, diamonds, emeralds and sapphires (RCIN 200140)
• *The Queen and members of the Royal Family including The Duke and Duchess of Cambridge gather for the Christening of Prince George of Cambridge, St James's Palace, 23 October 2013.* Photograph by Jason Bell © Camera Press

p. 112
• *Queen Elizabeth The Queen Mother and The Queen on the balcony of Buckingham Palace on Queen Elizabeth's one hundredth birthday, 4 August 2000.* Photograph by Jeff Moore (RCIN 2999977). Royal Collection Trust/All Rights Reserved

• Congratulatory telegram, with envelope, sent by The Queen to Queen Elizabeth on her hundredth birthday, 4 August 2000 (RA QEQM/PRIV/CSP/FAM)
• *Crowds gather around the Queen Victoria Memorial in the Mall to watch members of the Royal Family appear on the balcony of Buckingham Palace as part of the celebrations of Queen Elizabeth's one hundredth birthday, 4 August 2000.* Press Association Images

p. 113
• *Eightieth birthday portrait of HM The Queen, February 2006.* Photograph by Jane Bown (RCIN 2999843) Camera Press

p.115
• Gold brooch set with precious and semi-precious stones, presented to The Queen in Columbo, 1981 (RCIN 250035)

p.116
• Shell plaque presented to The Queen in the Bahamas, 1985 (RCIN 72553)

p.117
• Gold brooch in the form of a porcupine, presented to The Queen in Ghana, 1972 (RCIN 250036)

p.118
• Painted tin model of a truck, presented to The Queen in Pakistan, 1997 (RCIN 94453)

p.119
• Norman Hartnell evening gown worn by The Queen to the opening of the Sydney Opera House, 1973. (RCIN 100038)

p.121
The Queen attending a concert on her State Visit to the Netherlands, 25 March 1958. Press Association Images
The Queen at Margam Country Park, Port Talbot, Wales, 26 April 2012. Rex Features

Written by Leah Kharibian and Jane Roberts

Published 2015 by Royal Collection Trust
York House
St James's Palace
London SW1A 1BQ

Royal Collection Trust / © HM Queen Elizabeth II 2015

100269

ISBN 978 1 909741 28 7

British Library Cataloguing Data:
A catalogue record for this book is available from the British Library.

Designed by Briony Hartley
Typeset in Weiss
Printed and bound by Printer Trento S.r.l.
Printed on Gardamatt Art 150gsm
Production by Debbie Wayment

MIX
Paper from
responsible sources
FSC® C015829
www.fsc.org